CRJ

KU-411-809

D1426987

WITHDRAWN

A000 000 001 9401

ABERDEEN LIBRARIES

discover countries

Kenya

Chris Ward

WAYLAND

First published in 2009 by Wayland
Copyright Wayland 2009
This paperback edition published in 2010 by Wayland

Wayland
Hachette Children's Books
338 Euston Road
London NW1 3BH

Wayland Australia
Level 17/207 Kent Street,
Sydney, NSW 2000

All rights reserved

Concept design: Jason Billin
Editor: Susan Crean
Designer: Paul Manning
Consultant: Rob Bowden

Produced for Wayland by
White-Thomson Publishing Ltd

www.wtpub.co.uk
+44 (0)845 362 8240

British Library Cataloguing in Publication Data

Ward, Chris
Kenya. - (Discover countries)
1. Kenya - Geography - Juvenile literature
I. Title
916.7'62

ISBN: 9780750264112

Printed in Malaysia
Wayland is a division of Hachette Children's Books
an Hachette UK company
www.hachette.co.uk

916.762

All data in this book was researched in late 2008
and has been collected from the latest sources available at that time.

Picture credits

1, EASI-Images/Chris Fairclough; 3 (top), EASI-Images/Rob Bowden; 3 (bottom), EASI-Images/Chris Fairclough; 5, EASI-Images/Rob Bowden;
6, EASI-Images/Rob Bowden; 7, EASI-Images/Rob Bowden; 8, EASI-Images/Chris Fairclough; 9, iStockphoto/Veronica Donnelly;
10 iStockphoto/Josh Webb; 11, EASI-Images/Rob Bowden; 12, EASI-Images/Chris Fairclough; 13, EASI-Images/Chris Fairclough;
14, EASI-Images/Chris Fairclough; 15, EASI-Images/Rob Bowden; 16, EASI-Images/Rob Bowden; 17, EASI-Images/Chris Fairclough;
18, EASI-Images/Rob Bowden; 19, EASI-Images/Rob Bowden; 20, EASI-Images/Chris Fairclough; 21 EASI-Images/Rob Bowden;
22, EASI-Images/Roy Maconachie; 23, EASI-Images/Rob Bowden; 24, EASI-Images/Rob Bowden; 25, EASI-Images/Chris Fairclough;
26, Shutterstock/Roca; 27, Shutterstock/Franck Camhi; 28, iStockphoto/Liz Leyden; 29, Shutterstock/Ewan Chesser
Cover images, Shutterstock/Paul Banton (left), EASI-Images/Chris Fairclough (right)

Contents

Discovering Kenya

Kenya, a country in East Africa, is known for its amazing wildlife, stunning landscapes and varied ethnic groups. Of Africa's 56 countries, Kenya had the tenth-wealthiest economy and eighth-biggest population in 2007.

Key features

Kenya is more than twice the size of the UK. Its coastline lies along the Indian Ocean. Kenya has Africa's second-highest mountain, Mt Kenya, which is 5,199 m (17,057 ft) high. Part of Africa's largest lake, Lake Victoria, is located in Kenya, too. This lake is almost the same size as Ireland!

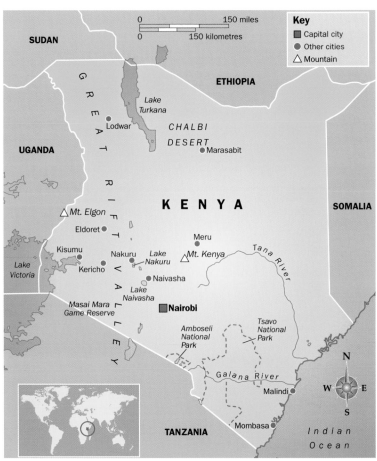

Running through the middle of Kenya is the world's largest natural feature – the Great Rift Valley. It is so-called because the land in this part of Africa is slowly moving apart, creating the rift.

A free Kenya

Kenya was a British colony from 1895 until 1963. Many Kenyans fought against control of their country by the British. After several years of struggle they won

Kenya Statistics

Area: 582,650 sq km (224,962 sq miles)

Capital city: Nairobi

Government type: Republic

Bordering countries: Ethiopia, Somalia, Sudan, Tanzania, Uganda

Currency: Kenyan shilling

Language: English (official), Kiswahili (official), numerous indigenous languages

independence for Kenya in 1963. Today, Kenya is a republic, so its citizens vote for government officials. Kenya's government is based in the capital city, Nairobi.

Keeping the peace

Since Kenya won its independence, it has been one of Africa's strongest and most peaceful countries. However, recent fighting between different ethnic groups led to the killing of hundreds of Kenyans. The fighting started during Kenya's elections in 2007 because different groups could not agree on how to best run the country. Today, Kenya is peaceful again, and life has returned to normal.

DID YOU KNOW?
At its widest point in Kenya, the Great Rift Valley is 320 km (200 miles) wide. To get from one side to the other, you would have to cross 629 bridges the length of San Francisco's Golden Gate Bridge!

▼ The Kenyan capital, Nairobi, is a modern, busy city. It is one of the most important business centres in Africa.

Landscape and climate

Kenya's landscapes attract tourists from around the world and are home to some of the largest populations of wildlife on Earth.

Tropical coast

Kenya's coastline stretches 536 km (333 miles) along the warm waters of the Indian Ocean. Most of the beaches are sandy. Coral reefs off the coast hold hundreds of kinds of fish.

▼ Palm trees are among the many tropical plants that grow along Kenya's hot and humid coastline.

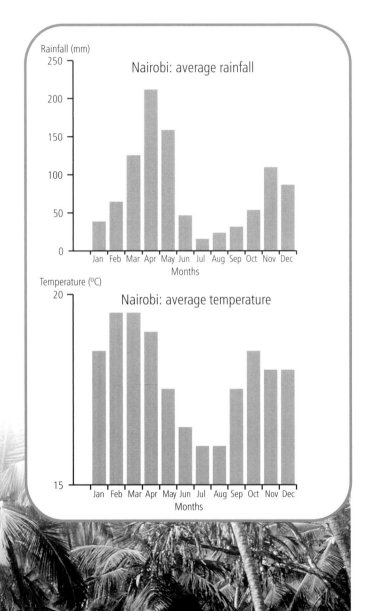

Highlands

Much of Kenya is highlands, where temperatures are much cooler than along the coast. It can be close to freezing at night. The highlands have regular rainfall and good soils and many of Kenya's farms are found in this area. Kenya's main highlands are found on either side of the Great Rift Valley. Kenya's highest points are Mt Kenya, in the centre of the country, and Mt Elgon, on the border with Uganda.

Lowlands and lakes

Kenya has several lowland areas, each with its own climate. The lowland area around Lake Victoria has a high rainfall and is very warm. Some of Kenya's best farmland is found here. The lowlands along the border with Tanzania are mainly grasslands known as savannah. This is where most of Kenya's wildlife is found. In the north, the lowlands along the border with Ethiopia and Somalia are mostly desert. They have little rainfall and are extremely hot. The bottom of the Great Rift Valley is another lowland area. It is also hot, but has a more regular rainfall than the desert. There are several lakes in the Great Rift Valley, but only Lake Naivasha is a freshwater lake.

△ Lake Victoria, Africa's largest lake, is an important source of fish for Kenya.

DID YOU KNOW?

Even though Mt Kenya is located close to the equator, it is high enough and cold enough to have snow on it for several months of the year.

Facts at a glance

Land area: 569,250 sq km (219,788 sq miles)

Water area: 13,400 sq km (5,174 sq miles)

Highest point: Mt Kenya 5,199 m (17,057ft)

Lowest point: Indian Ocean 0 m (0 ft)

Longest river: Tana River 708 km (440 miles)

Coastline: 536 km (333 miles)

Population and health

In 2008 Kenya had a population of around 38 million people. Kenya's population is growing. There are four times more people living in Kenya now than when Kenya became independent from the UK in 1963. Almost half of all Kenyans are under 18 years of age.

Still growing

Kenya's population will continue to grow in the coming years. This is because many young people in Kenya have yet to grow up and begin families of their own. Kenya's population is growing by about 77,500 people every month, or 106 people every hour! By 2040 Kenya is expected to have around twice as many people as it does today.

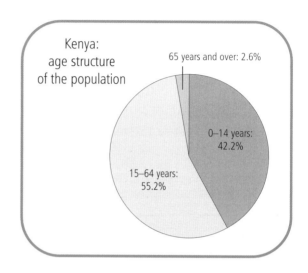

Kenya:
age structure
of the population

65 years and over: 2.6%

0–14 years: 42.2%

15–64 years: 55.2%

DID YOU KNOW?

Kenya's population is growing fast enough to fill a mid-sized aeroplane full of passengers every 3 hours!

🔻 Many of Kenya's people are young and the population is growing fast. It is hard for the government to meet needs for housing, health and education.

Mixed population

Kenya has over 60 different ethnic groups. The biggest black ethnic groups are the Kikuyu, Luhya and Luo. They make up nearly half of the population. People of Arab origin live along Kenya's coast and on the island of Lamu. They first came to the area as traders and settled there more than a thousand years ago. Europeans (mostly British) arrived when Kenya was a colony. Some remained when Kenya became independent. Indians also came to Kenya when it was a colony. They were brought over by the British to help build the railway. Many have settled in towns along the main railway route, such as Mombasa, Nairobi and Kisumu.

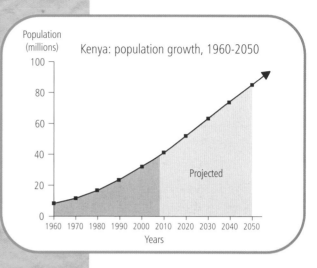

Kenya: population growth, 1960-2050

Health and poverty

Kenya's main health problems are caused by poverty and a lack of access to education or medical facilities. The drinking of dirty water is the main cause of illness and death in Kenya. Malaria is one of Kenya's most serious diseases. It is passed to humans when they are bitten by mosquitoes carrying the disease. Teaching people how to avoid mosquito bites, such as by sleeping under a mosquito net, can help to stop them from getting the disease. Many Kenyan's have died from AIDS, a disease first discovered in the 1980s that has no cure.

Facts at a glance

Total population: 38 million
Life expectancy at birth: 56.6
Children dying before the age of five: 12.1 %
Ethnic composition: Kikuyu 21%, Luhya 14% Luo 13%, Kalenjin 11%, Kamba 11%, Gusii 6%, Meru 5%, other 19%

▶ Surgeons operate in a modern Kenyan hospital. Most of Kenya has only basic health facilities.

Settlements and living

About 80 per cent of Kenyans live in rural areas, but this is changing. Some people have left villages to find jobs in towns or cities. The way people live in Kenya is also changing.

Urban growth

Kenya's towns and cities are growing quickly. Nairobi's population increased from 1 million in 1985 to 3 million in 2007. By 2025 it is expected to grow to nearly 6 million. Nairobi is growing so fast that there are not enough homes for everyone. Many people live in makeshift homes made from old bits of metal or wood in slums, or shanty towns. Mathare slum in Nairobi has over half a million people. It is one of the largest slums in the world.

Kenya's other main cities are Mombasa, on the coast, and Kisumu, near Lake Victoria. They are also growing fast, but not as quickly as Nairobi. Mombasa and Kisumu each have fewer than 1 million people.

Facts at a glance

Urban population:
21% (8 million)

Rural population:
79% (30 million)

Population of largest city:
3 million (Nairobi)

🔻 Homes in slums, or shanty towns, often have no water, toilets or electricity.

Rich and poor

More than half of all Kenyans live in poverty, but there are some wealthy people in Kenya. They enjoy lifestyles similar to rich people in Europe or the USA. They visit smart shops and eat in expensive restaurants. They have modern cars and live in large private homes, often with servants and gardeners. Most Kenyans are poor, however. Around 23 per cent of the population survives on less than US$1 per day. Poor people in cities live in small rented homes or slums. In rural areas, their homes are often simple buildings.

On the move

Pastoralists are people who keep animals such as cattle, goats and sheep. In Kenya, some pastoralists travel long distances with their animals to find fresh grass or water. They may be away from home for many weeks and live in temporary shelters. Some pastoralists are nomadic and have no permanent home at all. When the grass or water run out, they pack up all their belongings and travel to another source.

● In rural areas of Kenya, homes are often simple mud and thatch structures. They can be quite isolated, such as this home on the edge of the Great Rift Valley.

DID YOU KNOW?

Some pastoral groups in Kenya live so far from towns that they may have to walk more than 50 km (30 miles) simply to visit the nearest doctor!

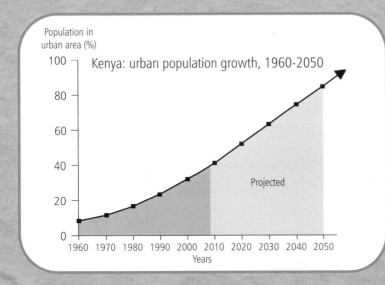

Kenya: urban population growth, 1960-2050

Population in urban area (%)

Projected

Years

Family life

In the past, Kenyan families lived and worked in the same village. In some places this still happens, but many families are now split apart.

Living apart

Kenyan families often live apart in order to find work. Family members may work as labourers on large farms or in factories based in Kenya's cities. People working in tourism might live away from their families for long periods. Children may also live away from their families in order to go to school. Many of Kenya's best schools are boarding schools.

🔺 Family life is important in Kenya, and spending time with one another is often linked to eating.

In Kenya, the family is still important, even when it is split apart. People travel home as often as possible and send money home to help support the rest of the family.

Helping out

Children who live at home often help out around the family home. Their jobs might include looking after younger children or helping with cooking and cleaning. Errands such as shopping and taking messages are also common jobs.

Facts at a glance

Average children per childbearing woman:
5.0 children

Average household size:
4.4 people

Some jobs are more difficult. Collecting water or fuelwood can involve walking several kilometres with a heavy load. Helping on the family farm can also be hard work, especially at busy times, such as harvesting.

Hard life

Women have an especially hard life in Kenya. They traditionally care for children and look after the family home. But they may also work on the family farm or take extra crops to sell in markets. Even women in paid jobs often have to carry on with their traditional roles as well.

Changing families

In the past people had many children because it was common for some to die while they were still young. In addition, families needed more children to work on family farms. Better healthcare means that today fewer children die. They are also not needed as much for working, especially in towns and cities. For this reason, family sizes are falling in Kenya. In cities, families may now have just two or three children. In rural areas, however, families with six or more children are still quite common.

DID YOU KNOW?

The men in some ethnic groups in Kenya may marry more than one wife. Their families might have over twenty children.

▶ A young girl cares for her younger brother. Many children help their parents around the home or by caring for younger children.

Religion and beliefs

Kenya's traditional beliefs are closely linked to the land and the worship of ancestors. Many Kenyans still follow these beliefs, but in addition they follow a major religion.

Christianity

About 80 per cent of Kenyans are Christians. The Portuguese were the first to bring Christianity to Kenya when they arrived in Mombasa in the fifteenth century. It spread more widely in the nineteenth century when missionaries came to Kenya from Europe. They set up schools and hospitals in Kenya as well as teaching Christianity.

Many Kenyan schools and hospitals are still run by missionaries today, especially in remote areas of the country. African churches that mix Christianity with traditional beliefs have become popular since Kenya became independent.

Kenya: major religions

Other: 13.4%

Muslim: 7.3%

Christian: 79.3%

▼ Most Kenyans are Christian, including these members of the Masai tribe in southern Kenya.

Islam

Islam came to Kenya through Arab traders from across the Indian Ocean. About seven per cent of Kenyans now follow Islam. Many of them live along Kenya's coast and especially around Mombasa. Nairobi also has a large Muslim population. Jamia mosque, the largest in Kenya, is found in the centre of Nairobi.

Other religions

When people from India came to work on building Kenya's railways, they brought the Sikh, Hindu and Jain faiths with them. Because some Indians chose to settle in Kenya, these religions are still followed by their descendants today. Most followers of these religions live in Nairobi, Mombasa or Kisumu.

Healers and witchcraft

Before modern medicines were brought to Kenya, people would visit a local healer. The healer would use plants, animal parts and minerals to make medicines. Many Kenyans still visit traditional healers today. Healers are often cheaper and easier to find than modern medical care. Some healers are also said to be witch doctors. Some believe they have the power to put curses on people and bring them bad luck.

DID YOU KNOW? The neem tree that grows in Kenya has so many uses that it is known as the miracle tree. Its twigs are used as toothbrushes. Its leaves cure stomach-ache. It is also a natural insecticide and keeps away mosquitoes.

▶ A boy from the Pokot ethnic group in western Kenya takes part in a rite of passage into manhood. He will have to prove his skills in hunting and survival.

Education and learning

Kenya has a good education system. One of Africa's best universities is located in Nairobi. Basic schooling is free. However, this simply means that the government will pay for a teacher and school building, but not any other expenses involved in going to school.

Facts at a glance

Children in primary school:
Male 78%, female 79%

Children in secondary school:
Male 42%, female 42%

Literacy rate (over 15 years):
85.1%

The cost of learning

Most Kenyan children must buy their own books, pens and uniforms before they can go to school. Other costs include travel and lunches. Some parents may be asked to help pay for desks or other equipment.

Many poor families struggle to meet the cost of sending children to school and may choose not to send their children to school at all. Other children may have to drop out of school if the family runs out of money. Families that can afford to pay the fees may send their children to private school. In Kenya, most of these are boarding schools that started as missionary schools. Some are still run by the church today.

▼ These children sit in a cramped and poorly equipped classroom in rural Kenya. Many schools in Kenya are overcrowded.

Mixed system

Around 80 per cent of children go to primary school in Kenya, but only 42 per cent of children go to secondary school. An equal number of boys and girls go to school in Kenya. Some private schools only allow boys or girls, but most are mixed schools.

Universities and colleges

Kenya has six public universities and around seventeen private ones. The University of Nairobi is the largest in the country with more than 30,000 students! As well as universities, Kenya has hundreds of colleges. They teach courses such as carpentry, mechanics, hairdressing and computer skills.

The cost of courses means many people cannot afford them. Some charities offer money to help students pay for courses. Charities may also run their own courses for a lower cost or even for free.

DID YOU KNOW?

Jua kali, meaning 'under the sun', is the local name for skilled wood or metal workers. Experienced *jua kalis* train others and pass on their skills, a bit like an apprenticeship.

⬤ A boy learns to repair bicycles. Many skills that are needed in Kenya are taught outside of the main school system.

Employment and economy

Kenya's economy is one of the richest in Africa, but is not very wealthy in global terms. In 2007 it was 102 times smaller than the UK economy and 543 times smaller than that of the USA.

A risky economy

Kenya's economy relies heavily on tourism and tea production. A change in world tea prices or a poor harvest can therefore have a big impact. A fall in tourism is especially damaging. This is because it is not only jobs in hotels that might be at risk. The jobs of cleaners, drivers, cooks, guides and souvenir sellers who provide services to tourists are also at risk. In 2007 the violence that followed Kenya's elections led to a fall in tourist visitors. Thousands of jobs were lost and Kenya's economy suffered badly.

A stronger economy

Kenya is trying to build a stronger economy by encouraging new business activities. For example, the manufacturing of household goods and food products has increased greatly in Kenya. New types of farming have also developed, such as the growing of flowers. This new business activity now employs around 60,000 people in Kenya. After tourism and tea, flowers are now Kenya's most important business. Kenya is promoting new types of tourism that are owned

This factory in Kericho is processing tea for export to countries around the world.

Facts at a glance

Contributions to GDP:
agriculture: 23.8%
industry: 16.7%
services: 59.5%
Labour force:
agriculture: 75%
industry and services: 25%
Female labour force:
43.6% of total
Unemployment rate: 40%

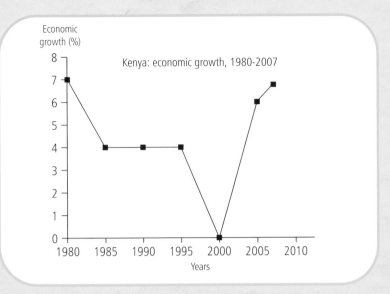

Kenya: economic growth, 1980-2007

DID YOU KNOW?

Around one in four of all the flowers bought for Valentine's Day in the UK come from flower farms in Kenya.

and run by local communities. These are known as community tourism or eco-tourism and mean that more of the money spent by tourists goes directly to local people.

Unemployment

It is very difficult to measure how many people work in Kenya. Many people work on small family farms. They produce food for their families and perhaps a little extra to sell. Because they do not work for anyone, these people are often thought to be out of work. Another group whose work is not official are those who do not have a regular job, but who offer services such as shoe-shining, tailoring or hairdressing. Unofficial work is an important part of Kenya's economy, especially in poorer urban areas.

▶ A man cooks snacks by a roadside in Mombasa. Many Kenyans do this sort of unofficial job in order to earn a living.

Industry and trade

Kenya has many small factories. They often use Kenya's natural resources to create products. Trade with other countries is very important to Kenya. Its ports provide the main import and export routes for neighbouring countries that do not have access to the sea.

Minerals

Kenya has small amounts of minerals. The most valuable of these is soda ash. It is mined at Lake Magadi for use in glassmaking. Limestone is mined in various locations and is mostly used for making cement. Another important mineral is fluorite. It is found in the Kerio Valley and is used in making steel and aluminium.

Processing

Some factories in Kenya process food. Kenya can earn more money for food items than it can for crops that are exported as a raw material. Vehicle assembly is another type of processing. Parts are imported to build vehicles for sale in the East Africa region.

Although Kenya has no major oil of its own, it has important oil refineries in Mombasa. They process imported oil into petrol, diesel and other products.

⬤ These red lakes are the soda ash lakes of Magadi. The water evaporates to leave the valuable soda ash behind.

DID YOU KNOW?

Kisii, a town in Kenya, is a source of a soft stone known as soapstone. The Kisii people use it to make pots, but it can also be carved into beautiful sculptures. Soapstone souvenirs are very popular with tourists.

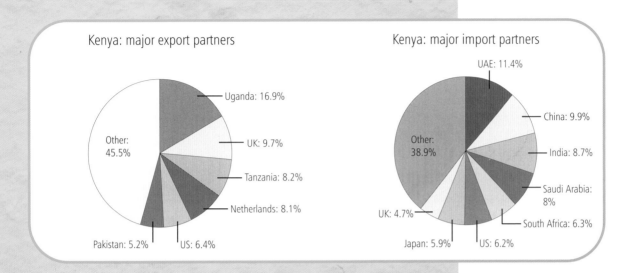

Kenya: major export partners

- Uganda: 16.9%
- UK: 9.7%
- Tanzania: 8.2%
- Netherlands: 8.1%
- US: 6.4%
- Pakistan: 5.2%
- Other: 45.5%

Kenya: major import partners

- UAE: 11.4%
- China: 9.9%
- India: 8.7%
- Saudi Arabia: 8%
- South Africa: 6.3%
- US: 6.2%
- Japan: 5.9%
- UK: 4.7%
- Other: 38.9%

Trade partners

One-quarter of Kenya's exports in 2006 went to the neighbouring countries of Uganda and Tanzania. Kenya has made agreements with these countries to increase trade. The three countries form the East African Community. Other important export partners are the UK, the Netherlands, the USA and Pakistan.

Kenya's imports come mostly from countries in the Middle East and Asia. Like many countries, Kenya imports an increasing number of Chinese goods. They made up nearly 10 per cent of all Kenya's imports in 2006, compared to less than 4 per cent in 2000.

🔻 A ship in port at Mombasa waits to be loaded with cement. Cement is one of Kenya's main exports.

Farming and food

Agriculture is the most important industry in Kenya. Around 75 per cent of Kenyans are involved in farming. Even in towns and cities, people grow crops or keep animals on any available bits of land.

Family farms

Most farms in Kenya are small farms that produce food for the family. In the south of the country, maize is the main crop. Millet and sorghum are grown further north as they grow better in the drier climate found there. Where there is enough water, rice is another main crop. Besides these main crops, a wide range of vegetables including beans, tomatoes, potatoes, carrots and cabbages are grown.

In the very north of Kenya it is too dry to grow crops. People survive by keeping animals such as cows, goats and camels. They buy the food they need by selling animal products such as milk, yoghurt and meat in local markets.

Facts at a glance

Farmland: 9.5% of total land area

Main agricultural exports: tea, flowers, coffee, vegetables

Main agricultural imports: palm oil, wheat, maize, rice

Average daily calorie intake: 2,150 calories

A woman collects beans from her land. Many families in Kenya have similar small farms or gardens to grow their own food.

Cash crops

Kenyan farmers also grow crops such as tea, coffee and sugar. These crops are called cash crops because they are grown for sale rather than for the farmers own use. They are often grown on large farms called plantations. The largest plantations in Kenya have hundreds of workers. Family farms may also grow cash crops if they have enough land.

Cash crops are mainly exported or processed into other products. Some plantations have factories that process the crops so they are ready for export. About half of Kenya's tea is processed in this way as well as much of its coffee.

Popular foods

Most meals in Kenya involve a sort of bread or thick porridge made from maize, millet or sorghum flour. This is normally eaten with a thick soup made with vegetables such as beans, peas, tomatoes and carrots. Meat or fish can also be added.

Kenyans' favourite way to eat meat is as *nyama choma*. It is grilled meat (normally beef) that has first been marinated in spices. Stalls selling nyama choma are a common sight in Kenyan towns.

DID YOU KNOW? Kenya is the world's biggest exporter of tea. In 2007 it produced 369 million kg (818.5 million lb) of tea – enough to make around 165 billion cups of tea!

○ Drought can threaten the hotter and drier regions of Kenya and can lead to food shortages. These people are collecting supplies from a food relief centre in western Kenya.

Transport and communications

Many parts of Kenya are difficult to get to. Many roads are simply earth tracks. They can become impossible to use when it rains. Transport and communications are better near Kenya's main towns and cities than in rural areas.

Road traffic

Roads are the most common way of travelling in Kenya. Buses take people on long-distance journeys, while heavy lorries are vital to Kenya's trade. The best roads connect farming regions and towns with Nairobi and Mombasa.

Most Kenyans are too poor to own a car. Instead they use shared minibuses called *matatus*. These are mainly used for short journeys in towns and cities and follow set routes. Large cars and pick-up trucks transport people and goods between towns and villages. They set off when they are full and will pick up people as they go, if there is room.

Facts at a glance

Total roads: 177,765 km (110,458 miles)

Paved roads: 8933 km (5,550 miles)

Railways: 2,778 km (1,726 miles)

Major airports: 5

Major ports: 1

▼ A passenger bus passes a heavy lorry travelling along the main road that passes through Kenya from Mombasa, through Nairobi and on to the Ugandan border.

Railways

The British built Kenya's railways to transport agricultural goods from Uganda and Kenya to the port in Mombasa. The railways have played a central role in shaping modern Kenya. Nairobi, for example, was founded when the British chose to build a rail storage yard there in 1899. Before that it was just an empty swamp. Other buildings were built around the storage yard and Nairobi grew to become Kenya's biggest city.

Today Kenya's railway is in a poor condition and is mainly used for cargo. There is one main passenger service between Nairobi and Mombasa. It has three trains per week.

Communications

Kenya's landline phone system is unreliable, so the use of mobile phones has spread quickly. The number of people with mobile phones grew from 0.1 million in 2000 to 11.4 million by 2007. Even poor people can now afford one. Internet use is also growing in Kenya, but not as fast as mobile phones. The Internet is mainly used by businesses and universities. Wealthy Kenyans who can afford a computer may also use the Internet.

DID YOU KNOW?

In 1898, during the construction of the railway from Mombasa to Nairobi, over thirty workers were killed and eaten by lions. The lions were eventually killed.

Kenya: Internet and mobile phone use, 1995-2007

Users (millions)

- mobile phone in use
- Internet subscribers

12
10
8
6
4
2
0

1995   2000   2005   2010

⬥ Bicycle taxis called *boda-bodas* are a popular type of transport in Kenya. They were first used in Kenya to transport people across the border with Uganda. Their name comes from the words 'border-border'.

Leisure and tourism

Most Kenyans spend many hours of the day working or travelling to and from work. This means they have little leisure time, but the time they do have is often spent with family or with work and travel companions.

What news?

One of the most common ways for people to spend their leisure time is catching up with friends and family. The Kenyan greeting *Habari gani* means 'how are you, what news?' in Swahili. This greeting is one of Kenya's most common phrases!

Kenyans often talk about family or work, but might also discuss sport or what is happening in the news. Newspapers and radio are very popular in Kenya. In rural areas, market days (normally weekly) provide an opportunity for people to catch up. Some people will travel over 20 km (12 miles) by foot just to catch up on the local gossip!

Sport and entertainment

Many of the world's best long-distance runners are from Kenya. Six of the ten fastest marathon runners ever are Kenyan men. Kenyan women hold two of the top-ten marathon times.

Football is the most popular sport in Kenya. Even Kenya's slums have football leagues. Mathare United is a team that began in Mathare slum. It is now one of Kenya's best football clubs.

Kenyan runner Philemon Kipchumba Kisang (in front) during the Milan International Half Marathon in 2008.

Music and cinema are other popular entertainments. Kenya has its own style of pop music. It is a mix of African, European and American styles. Most films in Kenya come from western countries, but African and Asian films are also shown.

Tourism

Around 1.5 million people visit Kenya every year. They come to relax on its beaches and to see its wildlife. A large wildlife reserve called the Masai Mara is one of Kenya's most popular places. However, it has so many visitors that there are concerns about the animals living there. Tourist vehicles can frighten animals and stop them from feeding or hunting. They can also damage the environment and cause pollution. Kenya is trying to encourage eco-tourism as an alternative. It limits the number of visitors to an area so that wildlife and environments are better cared for.

Facts at a glance

Tourist arrivals (millions)
1995   0.9
2000   0.9
2005   1.5

DID YOU KNOW?
One of Kenya's most famous tourist attractions is a restaurant called Carnivore in Nairobi. It specialises in barbecued meat including waterbuck, giraffe, zebra, ostrich and crocodile!

▼ Tourists view passing elephants from the safety of their safari vehicle.

Environment and wildlife

Kenya has some of the world's most spectacular wildlife. It also has landscapes that are popular for trekking and walking.

Big and small beasts

Kenya's grasslands are home to animals such as elephants, lions, leopards, giraffes, rhinos and buffalo. However, wildlife such as zebra, antelope and wildebeest are more common. Every July is the Great Migration. This is when around 1.3 million wildebeest arrive in the Masai Mara from neighbouring Tanzania. They come to feed on the fresh grasses that follow a rainy season. After a month or so they return to Tanzania.

The Great Rift Valley

Kenya's Great Rift Valley has many special environments. In the bottom of the valley there are several lakes. Some of them attract large numbers of flamingos. The lakes may even appear to be pink from a distance!

DID YOU KNOW?

Kenya is home to the world's fastest land animal, the cheetah. An adult cheetah can run up to 112 km per hour (70 miles per hour), but only for very short distances.

▼ Lake Nakuru in the Great Rift Valley is a soda lake. Its waters are too salty for human use, but attract millions of flamingos.

The valley also has some volcanoes. Mt Longonot is its largest volcano. It last erupted in 1860. Heat from under the ground in this area is used to generate electricity. This is called geothermal energy. It is one of Kenya's most important sources of power and is renewable. This means it does not harm the environment like using coal or oil.

Pollution and conservation

Air and water pollution are major problems in Kenya's towns and cities. In poor areas rubbish is often piled on the streets. When it rains, rubbish can wash into rivers or lakes and poison the water.

Burning is one way to clear the rubbish, but it causes serious air pollution. In rural areas, the clearing of forests for fuelwood or farmland is a problem. Removing the trees leads to greater soil erosion as the trees no longer protect the soil from winds and rain. The Kenyan government has set up reserves and parks to protect Kenya's remaining forests. It is also working with farmers to plant more trees. This helps to hold soils together and reduce erosion.

⬭ Wildebeest wander the plains of the Masai Mara during the annual Great Migration.

Facts at a glance

Proportion of area protected: 6.0%
Biodiversity (known species): 8,016
Threatened species: 164

Glossary

border the dividing line between two countries or regions

cash crops crops grown for sale rather than for use by a farmer; coffee, tea and sugar are examples of cash crops

climate the normal weather conditions of an area

colony a country controlled by another country; Kenya was once a colony of the UK

communications use of telephones, the Internet or the media (TV, radio, newspapers) to communicate with others

coral reef environment made up of the skeletons of living coral

economy the total of the goods and services produced by, and consumed by, a country or region

export good or service that is sold to another country

fuelwood wood used as a fuel to provide heat or light

GDP total value of goods and services produced by a country

Great Rift Valley a large valley that runs across East Africa; it is one of the largest landscape features on Earth

healer someone who is thought to have powers to heal people; healers normally use traditional rather than modern methods

highland an area of land that is high in altitude

Hindu someone who follows the beliefs of Hinduism, a religion originally from India

import good or service that is bought from another country

independence freedom from another government; Kenya became independent from the UK in 1963

industry any activity that processes or manufactures raw materials into finished products

Jain a person who follows the beliefs of Jainism, a religion originally from India

landscapes physical features (such as mountains, rivers, and deserts) of a place

lowland an area of land that is low in altitude

marinate to soak food (normally meat) in a sauce or spices so that it becomes more flavoured

minerals solid substance that is found in rocks or the ground; salt, gold and limestone are examples of minerals

missionaries people who travel to other countries to preach Christian beliefs

mosque religious building in which Muslims offer prayer

natural resources water, soil, trees and minerals that are found naturally in an area

nomadic a lifestyle that involves regularly moving

raw material an ingredient that is used to produce something else; trees are the raw material used to make paper

republic a system of government in which people elect officials to make decisions on their behalf

reserve an area of land that is set aside to protect the habitat, wildlife or people living there

rite of passage ceremony that marks a significant change in a person's life

rural relating to the countryside

savannah habitat that is dominated by grasses and occasional trees and bushes

shanty town a settlement that is unplanned

Sikh someone who follows the beliefs of Sikhism, a religion originally from India

sorghum a food plant that produces a grain that is widely eaten in Africa

Topic web

Use this topic web to explore Kenyan themes in different areas of your curriculum.

History
Kenya was once part of the British Empire. Find out what you can about this. Which other countries were also part of the British Empire?

Geography
Kenya is located on the equator. Find out what this is using an atlas. How many other countries are on the equator?

Science
Kenya produces soda ash by allowing water to evaporate and leave behind mineral salts. Find out how evaporation works and design an experiment to show it in action.

Maths
Find out how many Kenyan shillings there are in £1. Choose some items (e.g. bottle of water, apple, chocolate bar) and work out how much they would cost you in Kenyan shillings.

Kenya

English
Think of three questions about living in Kenya that you have after reading this book. Write a letter to a child in Kenya to find out the answers to the questions.

Citizenship
Kenya produces many food crops for export around the world. You and your family probably use some of these without realising. Why should we be more aware of where our food comes from? Do you have any concerns about buying food from Kenya?

Design and Technology
Many people in Kenya live in poor quality urban areas known as slums. Can you think of some low-cost designs that might improve the lives of people living there?

ICT
Imagine you are planning a holiday to Kenya. Use the Internet to find out when is best to go and what are the main things to see.

Further information and index

Further reading

Kenya (Letters from Around the World), Ali Brownlie Bojang (Cherrytree Books 2008)
Kenya (Welcome to my Country), Roseline NgCheong-Lum and Victoria Derr (Franklin Watts 2006)
Kenya (Living In), Ruth Thomson (Franklin Watts 2005)

Web

http://news.bbc.co.uk/1/hi/world/africa/country_profiles/1024563.stm
This is the BBC news page for Kenya with recent events and background information, including a timeline of major events.
www.oxfam.org.uk/coolplanet/kidsweb/world/kenya/index.htm
See Oxfam's Cool Planet pages for materials on Kenya.
http://ihs-198.magicalkenya.com/
The official Kenya tourism pages with a useful About Kenya section.

Index